THE BOOK
OF
GODS

DAVID G. MCAFEE

CHUCK HARRISON

KINDA BORING INTRO (FOR GROWN-UPS)

The Book of Gods is the second in a series of books for kids of all ages on belief, gods, and religion.

The first part of this collection was *The Belief Book*, which helps readers learn all about the origins of beliefs and why they are important. It also discusses the difference between supported and unsupported beliefs, as well as how our ancestors turned stories into beliefs over time.

You're holding the next piece of this complex puzzle: *The Book of Gods*. This work is published by Atheist Republic, but it was not written to teach kids to be atheists or to teach them that gods are somehow bad. It is to help them learn all about the different deities, their stories, and why we invented them. In the book, we delve into the rich histories of divine figures and discover how belief in them spread and in some cases ceased all together, all while encouraging everyone to come to their own well-reasoned conclusions.

We don't want to demean religion or cast belief in god(s) as something "evil." Instead, our goal is to promote religious education in a friendly and secular way to children, as well as to adults who enjoy simple explanations to these complicated topics.

That's why we broke this book up into three separate parts. The first part, chapters one through three, talks about how the gods came to be. The second part, just chapter four, introduces you to some of the most worshiped and popular gods in a trip around the world. And the third part, chapters five through eight, talks about how people worship, or do not worship, these deities.

We hope that you'll join us on this journey and the next as we discover even more about gods and religions and their places in society and history!

Never stop learning or asking questions,

- David and Chuck

P.S. Every illustration in this book has been drawn with your kid in mind. They're all able to be colored! So, when reading The Book of Gods with your little one, pull out some crayons or colored pencils and let them explore the world of the gods with colors from their imaginations!

David G. McAfee is a Religious Studies Graduate, a journalist, and the author of *The Belief Book; Mom, Dad, I'm an Atheist: The Guide to Coming Out as a Non-believer;* and *Disproving Christianity and other Secular Writings.* He is also a columnist for Canadian Freethinker Magazine, as well as a contributor to American Atheist Magazine and an editor for Ockham Publishing. McAfee attended University of California, Santa Barbara, and graduated with bachelor's degrees in *English* and *Religious Studies with an emphasis on Christianity and Mediterranean religions.*

"To Holly, who helped me understand and talk to children, and to every young person who has an interest in gods or religion. Never stop asking questions!"

Chuck Harrison is an illustrator and writer who lives with his son called, Puff and his cat named, Monkey in New York. His caffeine-fueled works have been published by DC Comics, Color Ink Book, Richard Dolan Press, and in many other fine publications. Everything else you may wish to know about him can be discovered at iLikeChuckHA.com.

"This book is for the first god I ever met, my mom. Without her tireless support, countless blessings and boundless love this book wouldn't be before your eyes. I'd also like to dedicate this to all the people out there who shared their love and encouragement with us, seeing your pictures and reading your kind words helped more than you'll ever know!"

TABLE OF CONTENTS

LET'S EXPLORE!

Welcome to *The Book of Gods*! In the first part of our journey that started with *The Belief Book,* we talked all about belief and why people believe the things they do. We also learned about different belief systems and how they came to be—and even created some of our own!

Now we are going to learn more about one of the most important human creations of all time: **gods**!

In this book, we will learn new and amazing things about all sorts of different gods and goddesses from all over the world. We will also find out about the very first gods—the really, really old ones—and where they came from. But most of all, we will try our best to answer some really big questions:

What makes a god a god?

Should I be afraid of them?

Where do they come from?

Where do they go?

Why are there so many of them?

Can we have ice cream for breakfast?

OK… that last one doesn't really have much to do with this book, but it's still a very important question. Sadly, for most of us, the answer is, *"No, you can't have ice cream for breakfast."*

But maybe there is a god out there who could bless us with ice cream every morning if we do what it says. A long time ago, people believed gods sent rain from the sky after they did a special dance. So, maybe we can make up a god who sends ice cream down instead of rain!

 2

The real question is: do you want to believe the ice cream is coming soon or do you want the ice cream to be a **reality**?

- Reality [ree-al-i-tee] *noun*:

- Something that is really happening; a thing that actually exists in the world.

*Dave and Chuck both love to read. Chuck likes fantasy stories about faraway lands, but Dave enjoys learning more about the **reality** all around us.*

That's really what this book is all about: reality. It's important to see how stories and beliefs are different from reality because, if you don't, you could end up believing in anything! When that happens, you might make important choices based on the wrong answers—and that's never a good thing.

What if you had a test in school, but you studied the wrong book? You wouldn't know how to answer the questions, would you? You could guess, but that won't get you far.

Or maybe you believe you can fly off the top of a tall building, just because you saw someone do it in a comic book or movie. How would that turn out?

A lot of people believe something magical happens with gods, just like with superheroes. They think our lives are like a game, and gods don't play by the same rules as the rest of us. In some stories, they can do just about anything they want—even bring people back from the dead or make it rain frogs from the sky. Some people even believed in gods that shot thunderbolts from their hands, changed into animals, and destroyed whole worlds with diseases or floods.

But have you seen any of this in reality?

You have probably heard stories about gods before—
they have been popular for as long as people have
been around, so that's not a surprise.

You may have heard of the Abrahamic god Yahweh
[Yah-we], the god of Israel, and his son Jesus [Jee-zuh
s]. And you might even know about another version
of Yahweh, named Allah [Ah-luh], and Muhammad
[Moo-ham-uh d], his **prophet**.

- Prophet [prof-it] *noun*:

- A person who is said to bring a message
from, or speak for, a god.

Dave and Chuck understand and respect the teachings of some religious leaders, but they see that in reality these are just people like the rest of us—not **prophets** *who speak to god(s).*

But even if you already know about these gods, you can still learn something new. Did you know that many of the gods found all over the world can get angry and sad, or be happy and filled with love, just like you and me? Even the most popular god in the world today, Yahweh, is said in the Bible to be "a **jealous** God."

- Jealous [jel-uh s] *adjective*:

- Feeling an unhappy or angry desire for what someone else has.

Dave and Chuck are **jealous** *of you because you get to learn all kinds of new facts about gods, prophets, religions, and more!*

We might think some gods are mean and would make really bad friends and even worse parents, but others still believe in them, love them, and follow all of their commands (or just the ones they like the best). And that's perfectly fine! People believe all sorts of things, and we should never **discriminate** against anyone just because of the beliefs they hold.

 6

- Discriminate [dih-skrim-uh-neyt] *verb*:

- To unfairly treat a person or group of people differently from other people or groups.

*Dave and Chuck might not believe in jealous or hateful gods, but they don't think anyone should **discriminate** against people who do.*

Some gods might be scary or mean, but others could be completely different. There are many of these *deities*, which is a different way of saying "gods," all around the world—including thousands you've probably never heard of. There might even be one who promises you ice cream. The only way to be sure is to learn about them all! And that's exactly what this book is about.

This book is split up into three parts. In part one, you get to find out how and why gods came to be. In part two, you get to meet some of them in a trip around the world. And finally, in part three, you'll discover how gods have helped to shape human lives for as long as we've been around!

So, if you're ready to explore, turn the page and take the first step on your journey into the world of the gods!

...Oh, and just between you and me, it's sometimes OK to have ice cream for breakfast.

THE SCARY UNKNOWN

We've already learned a lot about beliefs and about how they can make us feel safe, but now it's time to take a walk on the scary side.

Have you ever sat around a campfire with your family and friends telling ghost stories at night? Could you feel a chill down the back of your neck as you heard the scariest part of the story? Did you feel your skin go all bumpy and your heart beat faster?

Or maybe you remember one time when it was late at night, and you thought you could hear a monster breathing under your bed!

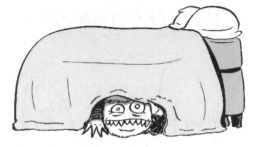

What's the feeling you get when you think about the monster? It's **fear**.

- Fear [feer] *noun*:

- A feeling we get when we think we are in danger or when something is going to hurt us.

- What we feel when we don't know something big and important.

*Dave and Chuck feel **fear** for the people who are discriminated against just because of what they do or don't believe.*

It feels weird, doesn't it? Maybe a little bit exciting, too? That's because this feeling called fear is just as powerful as belief—maybe even more powerful. Fear is amazing because it can change how people act. It can make them do or believe just about anything!

The truth is we all feel fear—it's just part of life. In fact, a lot of things in the world are based on fear. For as long as there have been people walking around on the planet, we have faced fear... and even used it to help us. That's because sometimes we need it to stay alive.

That's right: fear is a feeling that is needed for our **survival**.

• Survival [ser-vahy-vuh l] *noun*:

• How we stay alive.

*Dave and Chuck don't fear religions or gods because they know that these are just ideas that helped with the **survival** of many groups over time.*

People get scared for a lot of reasons, like if they don't

know the right answers to their questions. Here are some really important questions our ancient relatives asked, but couldn't always answer:

What am I going to eat today?

Where am I going to get the food?

Where can I sleep tonight?

How do we stay safe from other animals and dangerous plants?

You can probably answer these questions pretty easily—today we know we can get food from the store and we can sleep in our beds. But that wasn't always true. People who lived a long time ago had to think about all of these questions every day, and that **motivated** them to do all sorts of things!

• Motivate [moh-tuh-veyt] *verb*:

• To make something happen or to give someone a reason for doing something.

Dave and Chuck understand that people long ago were **motivated** *to get food, water, and shelter, because those things were needed for their survival.*

Everyone is afraid of something different. You might be scared that you'll wake up late for school or that you'll get in trouble for passing notes, but for a farmer hundreds of years ago there was probably nothing scarier than a season without rain to help the plants grow.

Imagine you were alive a long time ago, even longer ago than our farmer friend. Pretend you were around thousands of years ago when they didn't have fresh water or toilets, let alone cars or smart phones or the internet!

What would you be afraid of? Could believing in a god who will protect you help you deal with this fear? Please write or draw your thoughts. Remember that there are no wrong answers because you just have to use your imagination!

_____
_____
_____
_____
_____
_____
_____
_____
_____

Were you able to use the power of your mind to see what fear was like for our ancient relatives? Could you imagine how being scared could have helped those people protect themselves? If so, good work!

Even though humans have learned a lot of things over the last 200,000 or so years we've been on this planet, there are still many questions we haven't answered. Some of those unanswered questions can lead to a fear of **death.**

- Death [deth] *noun*:

- The end of life, when you aren't alive anymore.

*Dave and Chuck know that **death** and survival are all just parts of the world we live in, but some people picture Death as a spooky man in a black robe.*

Some people fear death because it makes them ask so many questions that they don't have answers to. These are just some of the important questions you or someone you love might have about death:

Why do people have to die?

What happens when we die?

Will it hurt?

Can we stop it?

Death is the end of life—it doesn't change. It's the most final thing you will ever see or go through. Once something is dead, it's dead and it's never coming back—and that can be scary. People fear this idea almost as much as they fear spiders or speaking in public to a bunch of strangers!

But if you're scared of spiders, you can stay away from them. And if you are scared to talk to a group of people, you can imagine them watching you in their underwear and make the whole situation seem silly. Picturing death in underwear is also silly, but doesn't do much to make it any less scary.

If that picture doesn't help, then what will? What do people do to make themselves feel better about death? Turn the page to find out!

WHAT COMES AFTER LIFE?

Life is amazing! Everything you know and love, you know and love because you are alive. But some day—just like everyone and everything else—you won't be. So what happens next? What happens after life? Do we turn into ghosts? Do we go to a really nice place? Or maybe there's a not so nice place?

The fact is that we don't know what happens after we die. No one does. There could be nothing, or there could be everything. Not knowing is what makes us scared, and what makes us **speculate** about what happens after death.

- Speculate [spek-yuh-leyt] *verb*:

- To think about something and make a guess about it.

*Dave and Chuck know that death is final on earth, but they still think it is fun to **speculate** about what else there could be.*

We don't know what happens when we die, but that hasn't stopped people from imagining and guessing. In fact, humans have come up with a bunch of different "answers" to this question. Let's see what stories Dave and Chuck have for us!

Dave: "I believe I will die and things will be just like they were before I was born. I'm happy with death being the final ending—I think this idea motivates me to get as much done in this life as I possibly can. If there is something after that, then that's great, too!"

Chuck: "When you die, you go to a dark place at first. But it's not dark for long; soon you find yourself in a world of pure imagination! Everything in this world can be controlled by you. If you're in a lovely forest but want to be in a big city, the world around you will change and become a big city. You can live here with your friends and family, who also have the same power as you, for as long as you wish."

Now it's your turn! Can you come up with your own version of what happens after we die?

As long as you used your imagination, you just did exactly what your ancestors did! But they went a step further. They didn't just come up with a story about what happens after death, many of them came up with "afterlives" that people still believe in today.

Most religious people believe in a good place, usually controlled by one god or many gods, where they will get to go live and be happy forever after death. These *afterlives* are a lot like the places we imagined earlier, but a bit different because there are usually a lot of rules you have to follow to get in. Millions and millions of people around the world believe that they have to do everything they are told by their god(s) to have the best possible afterlife.

Some religious groups call this happy place "**Heaven**," while others call it *Jannah* [ja-nah], *Paradise* [par-uh-dahys], or even *Aaru* [ah-roo].

- Heaven [hev-uh n] *noun*:

- Heaven is where some religious people think good people go after death. They say it is a place filled with God and angels and happiness.

*Dave and Chuck find it is best not to speculate about going to **Heaven** after we die. Instead they think we should work to make this earth our Heaven!*

But it isn't all happy news, because the best possible afterlife is only one side of the coin. With the good always comes the bad. When it comes to afterlives, sometimes the bad is the worst possible thing you can think of! Imagine the scariest thing ever and then times it by a million, billion, trillion, zillion! Yeah, the bad afterlives can be that bad.

In many cultures, this place—the opposite of Heaven—is called **Hell**. But other groups of people call it *Jahannam* [jah-heh-nam], and some call it *Tartarus* [tahr-ter-uhs].

- Hell [hel] *noun*:

- Hell is where some religious people think bad people and non-believers go after death. Many say it is a place filled with fire and pain and sadness.

*Dave and Chuck think that, no matter what people do on earth, they don't deserve to be tortured forever in **Hell**.*

People fear death and the unknown so much that we sometimes believe the stories we've made up about what happens after we die. This can make some of us happier, while others get more scared and even tell people they are going to Hell! But we know that's not true… and we know the people who say these things aren't evil; they are just scared.

Our fear of death and being gone can cause people to do other things, too. Many will obey the orders of gods they only know from books or heard about from family members—even if those orders are bad!

This can be a problem because, most of the time, gods have a ton of demands.

But if you don't believe in a god, you don't have to follow its orders! You can do the right thing for the right reasons and not because you're afraid of being sent to Hell. You can help and love people and do the best you can without thinking about rewards or punishments.

Now that we understand how fear can make people believe in gods and afterlives, let's find out how love can do the exact same thing!

LOVE FROM ABOVE

Fear can make people do and believe some crazy things, but so can love! Feelings are really powerful like that. And if we can understand our feelings, also called *emotions* [ih-moh-shuh ns], then we can learn more about why we do the things we do.

A long time ago there was a TV show for little kids. This was a very special show because its star was a giant, colorful dinosaur! Actually, he was a *Tyrannosaurus rex* [tye-ran-uh-sawr-us rex] and he was purple.

To make everything even more strange, this dinosaur loved you more than anything else on planet earth. He even had a song all about how he loves you and you love him, like a happy family!

Kids loved this dinosaur. He was their favorite thing to watch. They didn't care about how strange it was to have a talking purple dinosaur walking around with people and loving them instead of eating them. To them, he was their friend and they loved him right back!

Many kids loved this made up dino so much they wanted to do more than just watch his show. They wanted his toys, his books, his cups, his bed sheets, and everything else with his picture on it. They loved a talking purple reptile and because of it their parents spent a lot of money on all kinds of stuff. Some of those kids probably still have their toys all these years later!

Love is that powerful. It can make people do and believe just about anything because it feels so good and we always want more of it. Do you know of any other people or **characters** who say they love you as much as the big purple dinosaur does?

- Character [kar-ik-ter] *noun*:

- Any person or being who is in a story, book, movie, or television show.

Dave and Chuck don't believe in Heaven or Hell, but they still enjoy stories about them. They have morals, lessons, and good and bad **characters** *just like your favorite books or films.*

Kids loved the dinosaur because he was always there for them. He always promised to love them and he never did or said anything mean to them — kind of how many people picture their gods!

You might hear someone say that "God is love" or that "Jesus loves you," but what does that really mean? Does Jesus love you more than the purple dinosaur does? More than your family does? How do you know?

People who believe might tell you that their gods love them — and they probably think that's true. But gods don't take them to baseball practice or throw them birthday parties or feed them every day, so why do they believe in that love? Sometimes it's because family members or "Holy Books," like the Bible and the Qu'ran [ko·ran], tell them it's real.

But why do those books say those things in the first place?

Love is a big motivator, just like fear, because it feels great to be loved and to give love. It's one of the best feelings we have, so it makes sense that it is a part of so many beliefs around the world.

Love has been an important part of religion since ancient people started telling stories about the first gods. Our ancestors knew they loved their families and that gods—who they believed created and cared for them—must be like family, too.

Imagine waking up all alone a long, long time ago.

You don't know what anything is or where it came from, but you know you have everything to keep you alive. The water you need falls from the sky, food grows from the ground, and you can even find a nice cave for shelter. If you heard a story about a man who lived in the sky and gave you all of that, wouldn't you believe in him and love him?

Now you know what was important for people a long time ago and what made them love their gods, but what would gods be like if they were created just for you? Feel free to write a story or draw a picture that shows some good things your god might give you today.

Did your god(s) give you video games? Your favorite toy dinosaurs? Something else? No matter what, you can now feel a little bit closer to your ancient ancestors. After all, they created gods the same way!

Love is a powerful thing. It's been said many times that love makes the world go around. The people who created the gods knew this just as you do—and that's why most gods are said to love whoever believes in them… and why people are still drawn to these gods today.

People believe in gods for all sorts of reasons, including out of fear and love. But who are these deities? Why do they do the things they do? If they're all so powerful, why do they need anyone to believe in them in the first place? The answers to those questions, and many more, are coming next!

GODS AROUND THE GLOBE

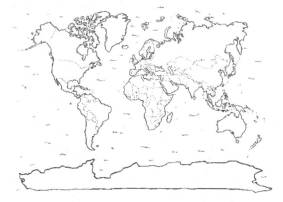

What is a god? This is not an easy question because gods can mean different things to different people. One person might believe the whole universe we live in is a "god," but other people think gods are more like people—only a lot more powerful!

For most people who believe in them, gods are the things that created or control humans. If these believers are right, it makes sense that every group of people would have the same idea of what gods are because they would all experience the same thing.

But that's not what happens. In fact, we see the opposite: some people believe in gods who live up in the clouds, but other people believe in gods who live on earth and have legs and horns like a goat! And other gods don't do much of anything at all.

Gods have been talked about for a long time—almost as long as people have been around! To get to know more about what gods are like around the world, we have to start at the beginning.

Who were the first gods? They weren't men with beards or half-goat people; they were the things people needed: the sun, water, earth, and animals.

Over time, because people love telling stories, these gods changed—they **evolved**—into much more.

- Evolve [ih-volv] *verb*:

- To grow or change slowly into something different.

*Dave and Chuck love reading a good story because they get to see their favorite characters **evolve** over time.*

To better understand gods and how they change between cultures and across time, we are going to take a trip around the world! We will make a stop in each of the seven continents and learn all about some gods who call them home. I hope you enjoy the ride!

North America

We start off on our voyage around the globe in North America, which includes the United States of America, Canada, Mexico, and more. Today Christianity is the most popular religion in North America, and Jesus and his father are the most well-known gods, but that wasn't always true. This continent has a history that goes back far beyond the creation of the Christian religion.

The Native Americans, the people who were in what is now the United States long before you or your parents or your grandparents were alive, had many different gods. These gods were mostly used as a way to worship weather patterns, plants, animals, and other natural things they needed to survive—just like we learned about earlier!

There were a lot of different native tribes in North America—many with their own special religions and belief systems—but one of the most popular Native American deities is just called "Coyote" [Kahy-oh-tee].

Coyote is known for being a trickster and for stealing fire and teaching people how to use it, but he was seen differently from tribe to tribe. Coyote was usually shown as a part-human and part-coyote god.

Coyote isn't the only Native American trickster deity. Some cultures also believed in Kokopelli [Co-co-pelly], a god of **fertility**.

- Fertility [fer-til-i-tee] *noun*:

- Being able to produce babies.

Dave and Chuck know that humans evolved over millions of years, and that we couldn't have done that without fertility! Our ancestors needed to have children so that we could be here today.

    Kokopelli is sometimes shown playing a flute. He is in charge of childbirth and farming just like Poseidon [Poh-sahyd-n], the ancient Greek God of the seas, is in charge of water!

Stories about Coyote and Kokopelli have been told for a really long time, but not all gods from North America are that old. New gods are created all the time!

The Flying Spaghetti [Spuh-get-ee] Monster (who sounds yummy) also comes from North America, but we just started hearing about this god in 2005 in Kansas. The spaghetti god was made up to make a point about teaching correct science in science classrooms, but today it is a well-known deity with a religion (Pastafarianism [Pas-tuh-fair-ee-uh-niz-uh m]) and word of worship (R'amen).

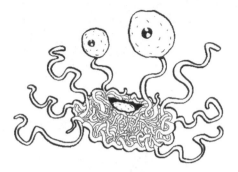

South America

Let's head down to South America, where (just like in North America) Christianity is the most common religion. Most people in South America are Catholic Christians and many of them worship "saints," Jesus, his mother the Virgin Mary, and Yahweh. We will talk more about saints and prophets in our next book all about religions!

South America also has many different gods that came before Yahweh. Most people who live there now are Christians, but the native people of what is today called Columbia believed in a Sun-god, a Moon-goddess, and more! They even have Bochica [Boh-chee-kuh], who they believed to be a hero who brought them laws and taught them right from wrong.

Bochica, like many South American gods, is often shown as having a beard or a "beard of feathers." He is best known for being able to teach and for the ideas he is said to have brought to the people who believed in him.

South America was also home to the Inca Empire, a large civilization that once stood where Peru is today. Inca mythology is made up of many stories and legends that have all kinds of different deities, including a creator-god known as Viracocha [Vee-ruh-koh-chuh].

Viracocha went by many other names, including Wiracocha and Con-Tici, but he is always thought to be one of the most important Incan deities. He is believed to be the creator of all things, including the universe and everything in it, and was worshiped as a god of sun and storms.

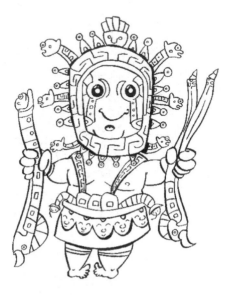

Europe

The next stop on our trip is the continent of Europe. We have to travel thousands of miles from South America to get there, but it's worth the trip! Europe is made up of about 50 countries, including Russia, Greece, France, and Spain.

There are a lot of gods that come from Europe, including at least one you probably know pretty well. His name is Thor [Thawr] and he is a Norse god who was believed to carry around a large hammer and control thunder and lightning.

Thor has been turned into cartoons and was the star of some big movies in the last few years, but he was created a long, long time ago around Iceland and Scandinavia [Skan-duh-ney-vee-uh]! He is known for his strength and he is said to be the protector of all mankind. Thor is the son of Odin [Oh-din], a powerful god of healing, death, and more. Odin is shown as having a long beard and one eye!

Thor, Odin, and Loki [Loh-kee], a shape-shifting god who also comes from Norse mythology and was made popular in movies, aren't the only European gods you might know about. The Greek gods are also from Europe and you may remember them, too. You have probably seen a TV show or movie with Hercules [Hur-kyuh-leez] and his father Zeus [Zoos] who lives in Mount Olympus, but there's even more to the story.

Did you know that there were other gods called Titans? They came before Zeus and his **pantheon**, which includes Hera, Poseidon, Athena, Hades [Hey-deez], and others.

- Pantheon [pan-thee-on] *noun*:

- A group of gods from a particular culture or people.

Dave and Chuck love learning about Zeus and his **pantheon** *because, just like people, the Greek gods evolve and learn over time.*

There were also some gods in ancient Greece who weren't considered part of "The Twelve Olympians." Hades, the brother of Zeus and Poseidon, lived forever in the underworld and was believed to look after the souls of the dead.

One of the most famous *Titans* is Prometheus [Pruh-mee-thee-uh s], who stole fire from the gods for humanity just like Coyote! This is a common story with gods because people knew they needed to use fire to cook and to stay warm, but they didn't know how they first learned to get it. They decided gods must have taught them!

In some versions of the story, Prometheus is punished for stealing fire by being sent to his own version of "Hell." He is chained to a rock on a mountain where an eagle picks at him every day forever!

Asia

Next we are off to Asia—a really big continent with a lot of people living there! Many people in Asia practice Buddhism [Boo-diz-uh m], a religion that doesn't usually have any gods, but that doesn't mean we can't find deities there. In fact, in Hinduism [Hin-doo-iz-uh m], a very popular religion in Asia, there are more deities than we can count!

In *The Belief Book*, we met Vishnu [Vish-noo], a Hindu god who is blue and has four arms. But did you know Vishnu is just one of many gods and goddesses from India? Other powerful deities in Hinduism are Shiva [Shee-vuh], a three-eyed god known as "the Destroyer," and Shakti [Shuhk-tee], who is sometimes called "The Great Divine Mother."

Shiva is the supreme god of Shaivism—one of the three most popular branches of Hinduism—and is said to be a powerful and fierce deity. Shiva is often shown as having a third eye and a crescent moon on his head.

Unlike Vishnu and Shiva, Shakti is a goddess and represents womanhood, female energy, and fertility. Shakti is the main deity of Shaktism and is thought by believers (called *Shaktas*) to be the force of all creation and the source of power for other gods.

India has a lot of gods, but there are many others that come from other parts of Asia, too. In Chinese culture, many people still worship the Jade Emperor [Jeyd Em-per-er], also known as Heavenly Grandfather, who is one of the deities known as a "first god."

Jade Emperor is said to be millions of years old and is believed to control all other gods in the area. Some believers say Jade Emperor created people from clay and left them to harden in the sun.

Africa

Our next stop is the continent of Africa, which has a lot of gods for us to choose from! The Yoruba [Yawr-uh-buh] religion in Africa has 401 god-like spirits called "Orishas." Just like we saw with the Greek system, there is a pantheon of gods and they are each in control of something different.

The first Orisha you'll meet is Shango [Shan-go]. Shango used to be a man and a king, but he was turned into a god over time. Just like Thor, he is a god of thunder and lightning!

Shango isn't alone. There's also Aganju [A-gan-joo], usually shown as Shango's father or brother, and Yemoja [Ye-mo-jah], the mother of all Orishas, who represents the spirit of women, fertility, and the ocean.

There's also Oba [Aw-buh], Shango's first wife, and many more!

There are lots of Orishas who come from Africa, but they aren't the only gods who call that continent home. There are also a lot of deities created by people who lived in Egypt long ago!

One of the most well-known Egyptian gods is named Anubis [Uh-noo-bis]. Anubis was a god of the afterlife in ancient Egypt, and he was shown as a man with a dog's head! Can you imagine that? We know about Anubis because of really old paintings from people who believed in him.

Australia and the Islands

We are almost to the end of our trip, but first we have to go to Australia to see what gods we can find!

A long time ago, before Australia was a settled country, the native people—called Aborigines [Ab-uh-rij-uh-nees]—lived there and worshiped their own gods and spirits. One of their most popular deities is Rainbow Snake [Reyn-boh Sneyk], which is given different names in different places.

Rainbow Snake, or Rainbow Serpent, is tied closely to water and to life, and is shown in many different types of art from the area.

Rainbow Snake isn't the only god of the Native Australians. Some aboriginal legends also describe Bahloo [Ba-loo], a "moon man" who keeps deadly snakes as pets, and a goddess of light and sun called Yhi [Yee].

In one story, we see Yhi try and fail to become close to Bahloo. This is why, according to the myth, the sun chases the moon around the earth but they never touch.

Let's leave the land down under and, before ending our trip in Antarctica, take a look at the islands of Polynesia. There are thousands of islands that make up Polynesia, including the Hawaiian Islands and Samoa.

You might remember the Polynesian deity Lono [Lo-no] from *The Belief Book*. In Hawaiian myths, he is a fertility god thought to be in control of farming, rain, music, and more. Believers in Lono thought he existed before the world was created and that he came down to Earth on a rainbow!

Antarctica

Well, here we are—our last stop! Welcome to Antarctica, the coldest, windiest, and driest continent on earth.

Antarctica is very cold and nobody really lives there, so that continent doesn't have any gods... yet. We hope you can change all that.

There are no people from Antarctica, but there are dolphins, killer whales, seals, and penguins—and lots of snow and ice. Maybe the penguins need a god who can help them get all the fish they need, or perhaps the dolphins believe they were made in the image of a god who could swim really fast!

Can you think of a god for Antarctica? You can write a story or draw a picture that shows your Antarctic deity and what he or she might do.

Did you create your god? If so, good work! I hope it can handle all the ice. If your god created people or the world it rules over, we can also add it to the growing list of creator-gods!

Here are just a few of those deities: Abassi, Abira, Adroa, Ahone, Ahura Mazda, Altjira, Amotken, Anansi, Anulap, Aramazd, Baiame, Banaitja, Batara Kala, Bathala, Brahma, Bunjil, Cagn, Cghene, Cocijo, Daksha, Damballa, El, Elohim, Enki, Eskeri, Gitche Manitou, Heryshaf, Huracan, Imra, Itherther, Izanagi, Jah, Karora, Kayra, Khnum, Kuk, Kuterastan, Lodurr, Mbere, Mbombo, Melek Taus, Muluku, Ngai, Nogomain, Noncomala, Obatala, Odin, Olelbis, Pacha Kamaq, Quetzalcoatl, Rangi and Papa, Tabaldak, Tagaloa, Tengri, Unumbotte, Vili and Vé, Xamaba, Yahweh, Zamba

Now that you've learned about gods from all around the world, and even made up one of your own, it's time to learn about what happens when people fight over gods. Turn the page to learn more! here.

MY GOD IS BIGGER THAN YOUR GOD!

So far gods don't sound so scary, right? I mean... they never really *do* anything, so why do people fight with each other over them? What's the big deal? Let's find out!

Think of your favorite cartoon or movie. Now try to pick the most exciting video game you've ever played, or the best song you've ever heard. These things are really great, right? Of course they are! That's why you love them. Now, if you want to, ask the people around you what their favorites are. We all have them, after all.

Do you have different favorites than the other people you talked to? Have you ever considered what it is about your favorites that makes you enjoy them so much?

Maybe it's because the characters are really cool. Or it could be because the stories really make you think… or make you laugh until you feel like your stomach is going to explode!

There may be a lot of reasons you love the things you love, but there is one thing that is almost always part of it. That thing is called **conflict**.

- Conflict [kon-flict] *noun:*

- A battle or area of disagreement; a struggle between people.

*Dave and Chuck know that **conflict** isn't always fun, but it is still in almost all of their favorite stories! Even in the happiest religious tales, the nicest gods of fertility, rain, and laughter have disagreements with others.*

No matter what stories you're a fan of, there's always some kind of conflict. Your favorite cartoon, movie, and video game characters all have a bad guy to fight or a problem to overcome. If these conflicts didn't exist, the stories you love wouldn't be as much fun, would they?

Batman has his Joker and Jesus has his Satan. One is good while the other is clearly evil. As a species of storytellers, conflict works as the glue that makes our stories stick together. Whether it's a person fighting with another person or having personal issues, or even a god fighting against another god or a team of gods, stories need conflicts to make them interesting.

SATAN ☆ JESUS

Now that we know what conflict is, let's bring back our favorites. What do you think is the best TV or movie character? Do you have a special sports team you like to root for?

Now imagine someone who disagrees with you is telling you that character is *terrible* and that your sports team is the *worst!* Do you feel the conflict yet? If you do, that's because something you *love* is being attacked.

Conflicts aren't just in stories. They are very real, and they come out when someone who believes in something strongly meets someone who disagrees. You see, most believers have a religion and that religion has one or more gods. Just like you and your friends will probably disagree about which superhero or video game character is the best, believers disagree about which god is the best or which is "real."

Sometimes people can be friends and "agree to disagree," but other times disagreements about which god is better can lead people to hurt others... all because they believe so strongly and care about it so much. Many wars have been fought for this reason. This is very sad, but it's the truth and there is nothing anyone can do about it. Or is there?

Maybe in the future people will stop fighting over which god is better. Perhaps one day we can all come to the understanding that it's OK to believe in different gods or no gods at all without getting angry about it! It's possible that people in the future will be able to put aside the hatred and just wish peace to those who believe differently.

If you're reading this book right now, you can be that change. You have the ability to others to have different opinions than you and not treat them badly because of it. You can change the world. How awesome is that? It's *super* amazing because, as you know, anyone who changes the world is a superhero!

WHY IS GRANDMA TALKING TO HER FOOD?

We all do some strange, silly things. But when a lot of people do the same strange thing, it is seen as normal—like singing in the shower or talking to yourself when there's no one else in the room. Can you think of a time when you've seen or done anything like this? I bet you can!

I bet you've even seen people talking to their food, too. Do you know why someone would do that? Maybe they think it'll make the dinner taste better? Well, believers don't see it that way. They will probably say they are talking to a god or that they are thanking a deity for what they are going to eat.

This kind of talking even has a name; it's called **prayer**.

- Prayer [prair] *noun*:

- A request to, or a talk with, a god; a hope or wish.

*Dave and Chuck don't say **prayers** because they don't believe in gods, but they also understand why believers do pray. The world is difficult, and conflicts seem easier to handle when you believe there's someone looking out for your wishes.*

Believers might say they are praying, but what do you see when you look over at your family members as they get ready to eat a big Thanksgiving dinner? You see them mumbling quietly to their meal. But because most people believe in gods and most people pray, nobody thinks this is weird at all!

Ever since people started believing in gods, they've been talking to them (or at least trying to). Most early believers made statues or "idols" of their gods and talked to them. They even gave these statues food and drinks and hoped the gods would bless them and their lands—something that many people still do today!

But some religions say you can't have idols, or items that represent their god(s). Instead of making statues of their deities, people who belong to those religions might pray to the sky or to the floor or into their hands... but the goal is the same. They want to talk with their gods.

Right now some of the most popular gods that people believe in are not allowed to be seen or represented on earth with idols, so that's why you might see a lot of people "praying" to nothing... or sometimes to their dinner!

If you're a believer, talking to your god or gods might make you feel good. When believers are stressed or worried, they can talk to their god(s) (or to themselves) and get it off their chest. And if a believer wants to help someone but feels like they can't do anything, they can talk to their gods and ask them to help. Even if the help never comes, the believer might feel better because they tried.

Some believers also talk to their gods because a lot of religions say that people are not all that great and that they are filled with **sin**.

- Sin [sin] *noun*:

- What religions say is bad; something that goes against a god's commands

*When some people do bad things, they pray to their god(s) to forgive their **sins**. But Dave and Chuck don't believe in gods, so they try to make up for their mistakes with real people who might have been hurt.*

People who believe in these religions are sometimes taught that they are "sinners" from birth and that they are sick and need help. What can help them? Well, gods of course! Not just any deities, though, religions say you need the help of *their* god(s).

Some of these systems tell believers that people aren't worth anything by themselves, and that they can't get good things on their own. The believers think they need to be thankful to their god(s) for everything they have, always. That's why grandma isn't *really* talking to her food; she's giving thanks to her god for giving it to her.

But you know a god didn't give that food to your family, don't you? Maybe you were at the store when they bought the groceries or you remember your parents working hard to get the money for them. Was there a god going to work every day? Do gods do your food shopping?

People do this with other things, too. When grandpa has a friend who's sick and he doesn't think he can do anything to help, he might ask for help from his god(s). When your aunt is angry with someone and does something mean to them, you guessed it, she might ask her god(s) to forgive her for acting like such a bad person. And the only way believers can ask for those things, the only way they can talk to a god, is to pray.

Now that you know all about prayer, you won't be confused when you see it. But not everyone prays, and not everyone believes in gods. You'll learn more about non-believers in the next chapter!

DOES EVERYONE HAVE A GOD?

We've gone all around the world and learned about a lot of different gods and how they want people to act. We've seen why there are so many deities in different cultures, and how people who believe in them use these gods to answer big questions or to make themselves feel good. We've even found out all about how gods can bring out the strongest feelings—love and hate—in people…

But what about the rest of us? What about the people who just don't believe in any gods at all?

The name of this chapter is a very interesting question that you probably already know the answer to: *does everyone have a god*? Even if you know the answer, it is a very important question that we have to ask. The answer, of course, is, "_No, not everyone has a god._"

Some people believe in one god, and they are called _monotheists_. If you believe in more than one god, you're a _polytheist_. But what about someone who doesn't believe in any deities? That person is called an **atheist**.

- Atheist [ey-thee-ist] _noun:_

- A person who doesn't believe any gods exist.

Dave and Chuck don't pray because they both happen to be **atheists**_. Instead of asking gods to help them, they focus on fixing problems themselves and thanking the people who really deserve it most._

Religions are all about _believing_ and, sometimes, those who don't believe are treated badly. This is a conflict, just like we talked about before, that comes from a disagreement over a strong belief.

If a theist (someone who believes in one or more gods) says a deity created everything and everyone and that it deserves our love, he or she might not like when someone thinks they are wrong. These believers are usually most offended by atheists, who don't even believe any gods exist!

For many years, atheists have faced discrimination for not believing. Remember earlier when we learned about how talking to yourself or praying might seem weird, but are actually "normal"? Well, the same thing happened with believing in gods.

Most people in the world believe in at least one god, so those who don't are sometimes treated as if they are bad or evil. Believers who treat non-believers this way are being unfairly **judgmental**.

- Judgmental [juhj-men-tl] *adjective*:

- Forming bad ideas of people too quickly; acting as a judge of others.

*Dave and Chuck try not to be **judgmental** of others based on their beliefs. They know that there are all kinds of people,* *including atheists, believers, and more, who do good things in the world.*

Does that seem fair? Should people who don't believe be treated worse than believers and even told they will burn in Hell forever? I don't think so! But many people do just that… so why?

To answer this question, you first have to name a toy or book that you have and love. Go ahead, we'll wait… make sure it's your favorite!

Now, did you pick one? Good.

Do all your friends have this same item? Probably not. Does that make them any different? Do you hate them for it? No way! Are you a better person for having your favorite toy or book? Not at all.

But the way gods get more followers is by getting people to believe, so religions sometimes teach that atheists are bad people or that they come from the Devil. It's sad that so many people think that because, as we learned earlier, an atheist *just doesn't believe*. Your neighbor or sister or dentist or mailman could be an atheist, and you'd probably never know unless they told you!

Some people believe in gods and others don't, but why? It can be for any number of reasons.

We talked before about how religions are passed on like stories from parent to child for many, many years. But sometimes that system fails, and someone just doesn't believe the story. What happens then? Sometimes the person is an atheist who has no good reason to pass on god stories to his or her children, who might be atheists too.

Other people start off as theists when they are young, and stop believing later because the beliefs don't make sense to them or because they think they are better off without any gods at all. This can also make someone an atheist.

A person might even become an atheist because they

no longer need the god beliefs that got them through tough times. Thinking someone else is in control can help some people feel better about bad things in life, but some don't need that at all!

So, if anyone can be an atheist, and atheism isn't a religion and doesn't have its own rule book, what ties all non-believers together? Nothing, right? Wrong.

What connects all atheists is that they don't have a god to look to for support or to ask for help. Unlike believers, atheists know that there is no amount of prayer or rain dancing that will change certain things in life. Atheists might even work harder in life to get things done or to help others because they don't believe in an afterlife created by gods.

We've learned a ton about gods and people who believe in them, and even those of us who don't! But what do we do with those facts? Can we use them to help people? Turn the page to find out.

'HIGHER POWER' RANGERS

A lot of people call gods "higher powers" because they believe these deities are in control. It's just like we talked about before: when we feel like we aren't in control, it is sometimes helpful to believe there is *something* in charge of it all—even if it's not us. So if gods are called higher powers, then what's a Higher Power Ranger?

A Higher Power Ranger is someone who knows all about beliefs and gods and can use that knowledge to help others. They know not to discriminate against people because of what they believe, and they understand why those beliefs might help some people feel better. Plus, some Higher Power Rangers can do awesome flying kicks!

With all this information, you're going to be ahead of a lot of other people in your understanding of beliefs and deities. By becoming a Higher Power Ranger, you can use that power for good instead of evil. You can teach people facts without being mean or rude, you can stop fights over differences of belief, and you can even grow up and write a book to help people understand better!

Now it's time for your first assignment, Rangers. Use your imagination to write a story or draw a picture about your job as a Higher Power Ranger. Are you going to beat up discrimination? Or save your whole family from false beliefs? Are you going to teach people not to be so judgmental? You can do anything!

Did you use your powers for good? If so, great work, Ranger!

We know Higher Power Rangers have a lot of power (knowledge), and that they use it to help others, but what does that mean?

Well, here's a list of things Higher Power Rangers might do: Read, write, draw, learn, ask great questions, help teach others, be nice to people, use the scientific method, look for evidence, form good (true) beliefs, respect the beliefs of other people, and more!

But what about the other list? The things Higher Power Rangers should never do? We have that one, too.

Higher Power Rangers shouldn't: Be mean to people who believe differently, hurt others, discriminate against anyone for any reason, act like they are better than others, call people bad names, insult anyone's faith, or call people stupid for their ideas.

Now that we know about gods and we are able to use that information to help others, what comes next? Turn the page and you'll see!

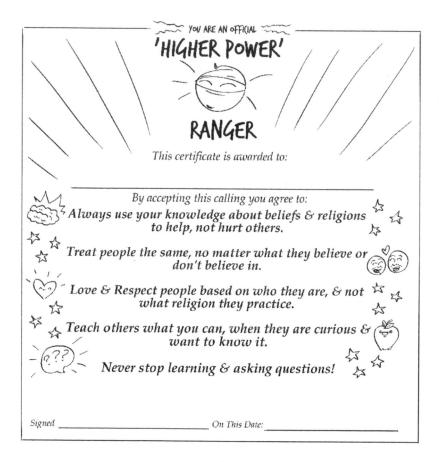

YOU ARE AN OFFICIAL

'HIGHER POWER'

RANGER

This certificate is awarded to:

_____

By accepting this calling you agree to:

Always use your knowledge about beliefs & religions to help, not hurt others.

Treat people the same, no matter what they believe or don't believe in.

Love & Respect people based on who they are, & not what religion they practice.

Teach others what you can, when they are curious & want to know it.

Never stop learning & asking questions!

Signed _____ *On This Date:* _____

IS THIS IT?

We started off our amazing journey by asking a ton of questions about what gods are and where they come from, and then we answered a lot of them! We traveled the world, but before we move on and head back home, we should retrace our steps and make sure we didn't leave anything out.

We learned about how our ancestors were scared of what they didn't understand and about how gods helped them with that fear, but we also learned that gods can be scary, too.

After that stop in scary town, we took a trip to the

"afterlives" of different belief systems—and found out why people believe in Heavens and Hells. We learned that there is no way to know what happens after death, but that people love to make stuff up!

On our way back from Heaven and Hell, we took a trip through the tunnel of love. We even talked about how feeling love from anyone, even a person or character that isn't real, can make us feel good.

When the love boat cruise was over, we took our biggest trip yet! We went around the world, to every continent and some islands, to learn about the gods and beliefs that are popular in each one. We even created a god of our own!

If you want, feel free to recreate the god you created in Antarctica or make up a new one! Can you make this god even better than the last?

Brr… it was cold in Antarctica! But when we got back, we found out about how gods and religions sometimes cause conflicts between people—and how to keep that from happening. This could be the most important lesson yet!

We were almost home, but we stopped by grandma's house to find out why she talks to her food. Now we know that's called "praying" and we understand why people do it! They are just trying to talk to their higher power.

When our trip was nearly over and we were almost back home, we took one last stop to think about how much we had learned and how some people don't have that knowledge! We found out how to be Higher Power Rangers and help save the world by educating one person at a time.

So what's next?

Well, we know all about the different gods and that believing in them helps some people but not others. And we understand that we should respect people and their beliefs even if we don't share them. So the only thing to do now is put these skills to the test. But how?

We say you get out there, and become a Higher Power Ranger! Invent your own gods and goddesses just like the creators of your favorite books, comic books or cartoons! Be happy and respectful and, above all else, never stop learning or asking questions!

In our next book, *The Book of Religions*, we will learn more about religions, prophets, saints, and holy books. We will find out what makes people hold on to their religion and how that grip can be broken over time. We might even be able answer some of the biggest, most important questions of all:

What makes a religion a religion?

Should I be afraid of them?

Where do they come from?

Where do they go?

Why are there so many of them?

Can we have ice cream for breakfast?

The next few pages are some extra space for you to create in. Perhaps you'll come up with all sorts of new ideas that you can bring to life on these pages.

Made in the USA
Monee, IL
20 October 2020